Departures

Poetry and Prose on the Removal of Bainbridge Island's Japanese Americans After Pearl Harbor

Departures

Poetry and Prose on the Removal of Bainbridge Island's Japanese Americans After Pearl Harbor

By Mike Dillon

To Mary Nelson (1926-2016)

& to the Island Where I Grew Up

The old ones who knew scarcity and war
slip away despite their strong grip.
Those who hear the ebb tide's hush
know a full cupboard was never a sure bet.

They slip away as forest and field topple
to the mixed-use mantra and roundabout
where maples once made sky-holes
luminous and blue as stained glass.

And so the old stories fade
like chimney smoke into a grisaille of rain,
or pages left open in a Book of Hours
abandoned beneath the noonday sun.

Table of Contents

In the Beginning

To be ignorant of the past is to remain a child, Cicero reminds us.

The imprisonment of some 120,000 people of Japanese descent who lived on the West Coast at the time of Pearl Harbor — most of them American citizens—now occupies its proper place in the historical record. When I was growing up in the 1960s, our school textbooks somehow forgot to raise the subject.

I was born in 1950 and was raised on Bainbridge Island, eight miles west of Seattle, where the first West Coast Nikkei were "evacuated" to Manzanar, a barbed-wire camp in central California's high desert. Later, most of Bainbridge's Japanese Americans were moved to Minidoka in Idaho.

Before the War, some 3,500 people made their homes on the Island's 27 square miles. Today's Island, with seven-times its pre-War population, is a high-end, Seattle bedroom community, thanks to an efficient state ferry system. The Island still has plenty of trees, and is very much a community, though it is far less diverse than the old, dirt-road Bainbridge with its roots in fishing, timber, strawberry farming and boat building.

Not until the 1980s did the underground conversations about the wartime imprisonments truly enter the public square. In 1988 the U.S. government apologized for its actions. In 1994 the best-selling novel, "Snow Falling on Cedars," and the subsequent movie, introduced the tragic and heroic aspects of the story to many Americans.

I am mindful of the late poet William Stafford's caution against "atrocity hunger"—appropriating the misfortunes of others as literary grist from a safe distance in time or place. I can only offer that what occurred on Bainbridge Island in March 1942, a little more than eight years before I was born, is part of my DNA. Growing up, I somehow knew that what had

I

happened to the parents and grandparents of my Sansei (third generation) friends had broken the Island's heart.

It's tempting to lodge a disclaimer at this point, advising: What follows happened long ago and far away. The political tides in this country and in Europe, however, remind us that a fault line running through the human condition—what the Greeks called *harmatia*—remains stubbornly perennial.

Saturday, December 6, 1941:
Bainbridge Island, Washington

In memory of Michele Antoncich

Dusk darkens the water's seal-smooth skin.
The old Croatian farmer,
a strong nave of a man built for storms,
rows out upon Eagle Harbor to touch
flame to wick in the harbor light
that guides the ferries in.

With mandarin calm, the first stars
come into their own.
Eight miles across the water,
Seattle's modest glow reddens a filament of cloud
where a freight train passes along the waterfront
with a faint, lathe-like thrum.

Wick lit, he admires the first festal lights
shining from the cottages
scattered around the harbor.
He crosses himself, as always,
dips his oars back into the sound of water
and rows for home.

There he will have his own wine to drink,
garnet as arterial blood,
and break his wife's warm bread
to christen the season of lights.
South, above Eagledale's dark firs, a star spills
from the wayside of infinity.

Adieu

After long talk of war and its alarums,
approximately 7:55 a.m. Hawaiian time
on a warm, blue Sunday
the bombs fell on Pearl Harbor.
Around 11:25 PST an Associated Press
radio bulletin informed the nation.

How many souls at day's end
secretly gazed upon a beloved face
from that secret place within
and whispered to a world
already being borne into the past:
"I shall miss you."

Remembrance: December 7, 1941

Monumental events, unlike the little things, come at us sideways.

A cod-belly-gray Sunday, with Christmas vacation only two weeks away. Out riding her bike with a friend, she heard people talking about a war. That is how most people first learned about Pearl Harbor—a glimmer, a hint. She'd never heard of the place.

Confused, she rode home and told her siblings about the talk of war. They switched on the radio. That afternoon and evening the radio streamed nothing but bad news as Japan advanced in the Far East.

The next day was school, a day in which the U.S. Congress would declare war on Japan. She felt anxious, but the teacher told the class that Japanese Americans were Americans; they had nothing to do with the war. Still, she felt nervous. As the days passed, her anxiety subsided.

For now, the boundary stones of the thinkable stayed put.

Wee Hours

"This is no time to mince words."

So wrote weekly newspaper publisher Walt Woodward in the wee hours after the Date Which Would Live in Infamy. Through the cold, dark morning Walt and his wife Milly prepared a one page, single-sided special edition of the *Bainbridge Review*.

"There are on this island some 300 members of 50 families whose blood ties lie with a nation which, yesterday, committed an atrocity against all that is decent."

After the cat's paw came the right cross: "I am positive every Japanese family on the Island has an intense loyalty for the United States of America and stands ready to defend it."

Already, up and down the West Coast, hatred stirred in its larval sac. And Walt and Milly Woodward stepped out upon their lonely road together.

Straw in an Ill Wind

In downtown Seattle, at Fourth & Pike,
a crowd of perhaps one thousand strong for whom,
in the ageless phrase, "alcohol was a factor,"
smashed store windows wherever a few interior lights
    were left on.

On this, the first night of blackout after a day of cold drizzle,
they went a-roaming in search of more lights,
found them and smashed more windows,
pausing, once, to sing "God Bless America."
A night blacked out like no other, but the mob
    required a deeper dark.

The Press

"I think it probable that, if Seattle ever does get bombed, you will...see some University of Washington sweaters on the boys doing the bombing."
— Edward R. Murrow

War dines upon our inner dearth.

And so a whirligig of furies took to the cankered hoof.
Even Edward R. Murrow, journalism's patron saint,
knelt as footstool for the Perennial Id
to mount the pale horse that leaps
our well-trimmed hedges unto ashen pastures
where the fisted heart pumps sulfureous wine
and little children mutter obscenities.

This, too, is an entry from the Book of Earth.

Remembrance: The Clock Starts

Another young woman came home from school to the surreal vision of two, big, black cars shining in her driveway. FBI. They searched house and farm and found nothing. They asked her father about contraband and he gave an honest answer: He had some dynamite for use on the farm. (Stumps still cluttered the fields of Bainbridge then). Maybe he was confused under pressure and misremembered: The agents found no dynamite but took him off anyway. Sometimes youth, on its own, sees through the world of appearances to glimpse a silver lining: She knew her family would take care of her.

Kimonos

Brightly printed cotton or silk
woven from patient hands
working quiet paths —

cast to the flames of their own making
along with porcelain dolls, old books,
calligraphy scrolls, phonograph records

and anything else that declared Japan,
If Truth is war's first casualty,
can Beauty be far behind?

From FDR's Pen

February 19: President Franklin Delano Roosevelt signs Executive Order 9066 creating "exclusion zones," the borders of which will be determined.

March 2: Lieutenant General J. L De Witt issues Public Proclamation No. I defining the geography of West Coast exclusion zones.

Bainbridge Review owners, like many others, think the exclusions include those of German and Italian descent — that this was an equal-opportunity exclusion: "The *Review* is glad it will strike all fairly without bigotry and without malice."

Not quite. Japanese Americans are targeted, even as their sons join up to fight. In a later edition: "There are many heartsick people on this island today...The *Review* — and those who think as it does — has lost."

March 24: Soldiers in World War I era, tin-pot helmets — naïve reassurance against the storm of lead building in the Pacific — board the ferry from Seattle to post Civilian Exclusion Order No. I: "Instructions To All JAPANESE Living on Bainbridge Island." They must be gone by or before Noon, March 30. Six days' notice, heralded by the sound of nails driven into wood this Lenten season.

Executive Order 9066

9066: Four numbers followed by the choicest words of judicial decorum:

whereas
therefore
authority vested in me
authorize
appropriate
excluded
impose
supersede
prohibited and restricted
duty and responsibility
such steps
action necessary or desirable

Square-shouldered words
upon which so much
depends.

Like the white picket fences
we put up between us
and the wind.

An Editorial

But we are talking here about 191 AMERICAN CITIZENS! Where, in the face of their fine record since December 7, in the face of their rights of citizenship, in the face of their own relatives being drafted and enlisting in our Army, in the face of American decency, is there any excuse for this high-handed, much-too-short evacuation order?

—Front page editorial, *Bainbridge Review*

Land

What we crave is reality.
— Thoreau

Abandoned farms to be cared for by Filipino farmers:
A decency made possible by lives defined
by the teeter of stewardship and struggle.

And so departing, weathered hands
reached out to weathered, stay-behind hands.
The vocabulary of the land held fast.

Were We There?

Taunts and jeers and hands locked
into fists coiled around the bent Christ.
We would not have mocked.

A curt knock on the door.
A distant, starlit braying of hounds.
We'd have rowed the slave to the other shore.

We know how the west was won.
We're not the kind to hood the inner eye.
Each day our human duty rises with the sun.

Anne Frank shelter with us?
Stout hearts must resist the sirens in the night.
History's arc is our sacred trust.

1941: The world rolled upside down.
Japanese Americans were our precious neighbors.
We know what we would have done.

But we weren't there — by luck or grace.
A moment of silence, then,
for decisions we never had to face.

Departure Eve

Three young breaths plume the dark:
my mother, her little sister, and their friend Mary.
They set out from their safe Wing Point world,
sift through the leafing woods and orchards they know
by heart with my mother, at sixteen, in the lead.

They come to an old house in a clearing.
The family, including a quiet boy, their schoolmate,
stands on the porch to greet those here to say goodbye.
Headlights flash up and down the driveway.
Hugs and whispers, sometimes tears, come and go.

The old grandmother in her rocking chair remains steadfast
as a bowsprit: She hands an orange to each visitor.
Oranges that glow in the starless night, just enough to light
the way home for my mother, my aunt and Mary
for the rest of their lives.

Concurrence

The cloud-covered moon two days short of full.

"Moonlight Cocktail," by Glenn Miller and his Orchestra tops the Billboard charts.

Eleanor Roosevelt, in her March 30 "My Day" newspaper column, will report a "beautiful" day after a quiet walk in the woods at Hyde Park.

The first mass transport of Jews from France arrives by train at Auschwitz-Birkenau.

Life Magazine's March 30 issue is in the mails. Cover story: "Shirley Temple Grows Up."

On Bainbridge Island, the Sabbath bells have been quiet for hours. An empty dock waits. Of sleepless nights, no count is taken.

Ticking

Monday morning, March 30

Remember hide-and-go seek —
that basilica of stopped time as we took
a last look around at our secret place
before a pair of hands juddered the hedge?

So they waited, counting the days
from Tuesday to Sunday,
then the Monday morning minutes
a moving knife's edge before a big truck's

growl in the driveway. A last sweep
of the eyes over the precious rooms
they would never leave. Then
a knocking. And not from the heart.

Remembrance: Pre-Departure

Another rememberer, a young girl at the time, came from a large family. All were American citizens. She remembered the heartbreak, the disorientation of not knowing where they were headed, wondering if it would be a hot or cold place. In fact, the place would turn out to be both in the extreme, depending on the polarity of the seasons. She remembered the feeling of being neither here nor there, the sense of security fading into the past.

Most humans aren't aware of what they don't know. Targeted families on Bainbridge Island lived in that nether world between knowing and not knowing — a piercing kind of knowledge.

The Dock

Plum blossoms bitten out against the gray.
Helmets. Bayonets. Rain threatens.
That's not what falls from certain soldiers' eyes.

High school has been let out for goodbyes.
My mother and grandmother stand in the crowd.
No one, not even the exiles know they are California bound.

The nightmare clock has ticked down
to this: the remaining steps to the ferry Kehloken,
the last patch of Island earth beneath their feet.

In Seattle crowds gather at Marion Street
waiting to watch the "aliens" marched to the train
for a journey to destination unknown.

In the Books: The Black and White Photograph

March 30

You think you can identify a man by giving his date of birth and his address, his height, his eyes' color, even his fingerprints. Such information will help you put the right tag on his body…war is the proper state for a world in which men are a series of numbered bodies.
— Thomas Merton, "My Argument with the Gestapo"

At the approach to Eagledale dock,
waiting with the rest under damp skies
to board the ferry Kehloken, she is dressed to the nines:
lipstick, heavy overcoat and small, velvet hat
as if bound for the city. The dignity of her gaze,
a brave prow turned to the waves, aims beyond
her sleeping daughter sprawled doll-like in her arms.

Each of their lapels has been stuck with a white tag.

She is indeed bound for the city,
waiting to be marched down the narrow dirt road
with the other white tags that evince
a blind lunge for clarity in a drunken world.
Sooner or later we will turn the page
and the beautiful faces of a mother, her sleeping daughter,
will fade like dawn stars above a dark wood.

Adagio

In the wheelhouse, Captain Wyatt of Bainbridge Island
assumes his role in a play no one understands —
authored by what malicious hand?
Tears fall from the captain's eyes.

The Island's low, green countenance fades.
No gravity-free, Olympian hand reaches down
to halt the ferry and gentle it back
to Eagledale dock.

That's not how the story is written.
Up in the wheelhouse, as the city draws near,
the captain's tears drop like silver coins
given back by remorseful Charon.

Remembrance: Transit

Sometimes the play of memory unspools honed, kaleidoscopic images.

The little girl who overheard talk of Pearl Harbor on that December Sunday while riding her bike found herself, with her family, at Eagledale dock. She saw the well-wishers who had come to say goodbye. She saw the tears. And then they were marched on board the ferry.

In Seattle they were marched off. She saw the overpass between the first avenue block and the ferry dock loaded with onlookers — an outdoor theater of expectation. The southbound train halted at its final destination the morning of April Fool's Day. Then buses drove about four hours along a winding, high-desert road to deposit them at Manzanar. They arrived just after noon.

Prescience

From Manzanar, a sagebrush camp of 10,000 souls,
227 of them Bainbridge Islanders, hedged by barbed wire
and the serrated Sierra Nevadas —
Island kids of high school age, on the *Review's* payroll,
sent news back to their weekly, hometown newspaper.

Weddings, births, deaths, gossip, youthful pranks,
beauty contests, softball league results.
To keep Bainbridge Islanders informed, the Woodwards said.
To keep their departed neighbors part of Bainbridge Island.
And to hold the gate open for their return.

More

Life goes on, is what we say.
How can it not? And humor,
prow to wave, never
takes a vacation.

One boy, object of amusement
back home for re-reading
his hoard of overdue library books
started up a new overdue trove
thanks to the jerry-built library
of Manzanar.

Another, because washtub
baths were banned,
walked a washtub to the showers
and sat right down in it
beneath the falling water.

Though another, in a letter
to a friend sent from the dramatic desert void
hedged by the picturesque Sierra Nevadas
leaned on the language of the visible
to make his life known—
he saw, he wrote, only the barbed wire.

Back home, meanwhile, the absence abiding
in the vacated houses and fields
made its way to thirteen empty chairs
set aside at high school graduation.

Manzanar: Just the Facts

Latitude: 36.7272° N.
Longitude: 118.1528°W.
Altitude: 3,727 feet.

Nine miles north of Lone Pine.
Six miles south of Independence.
Two hundred thirty miles northeast of Los Angeles.
County: Inyo.
State: California.
Country: USA

Inmate residential area: Not quite a square mile.
Population: 10,000 people.
Housing: 504 20'x100' tarpaper-pine barracks.

Climate: Extreme.
Summer temperatures often exceed 100°.
Winter temperatures: below freezing to low 40s.
        Snow not infrequent.

Security:
Guard towers with searchlights; barbed wire.
Tower guards armed with Thompson sub machine guns, shotguns,
        30' caliber rifles. Guns point inwards.

Manzanar: Spanish for "apple orchard."
Native Americans lived here for 10,000 years.
Discovery of gold and silver nearby in the 1860s led to their
        displacement.

Gaman[1]

From the concentration of hearts and hands
Manzanar's badlands gave birth
to beauty wrested from a universe
hedged by guard towers and barbed wire.

Woven baskets. Sumi-e paintings.
Ikebana's floral intersections of time and eternity.
Origami. Bonsai sculpted from the winds of the mind.
Carved walking sticks. Haiku poetry and wooden bird pins.

Condemned to send hope somewhere into the future
they chose to work their world at hand
where wind heaped sand into their tarpaper shacks—
and reclaimed an old alliance with earth.

---

[1] Gaman (gah-mon): *A Japanese word for enduring the seemingly unendurable with patience and dignity.*

Black and White Photograph, Manzanar: Rock Garden with Pool

A pool's face mirrors a sky empty of harm.
Around it white boulders are placed just so,
the way flowers are arranged sometimes.

You can almost feel the rough bark of Ponderosa pines
matched with desert flowers and clipped lawn,
can almost feel the smooth, white lean of aspens

as the pale egg of a day moon
floats above the near hills.
Barbed wire, from this angle, remains out of sight.

As do those other lands
beyond the mountains and seas where blood irrigates
the tight-lipped bone-heaps.

The photograph bequeaths a silence
down the years. Where the eye is quieted,
so are we.

Two Class Photographs

In the Bainbridge Island Historical Museum in Winslow, two large displays side by side showcase the Bainbridge High School yearbook portraits for the classes of 1942 and 1943.

The class of 1942 shots would have been taken in the fall of 1941. Forty-eight smiling faces. A fair many of them Japanese American.

The class of 1943 features twenty-eight faces — all white. My mother is in the second row from the bottom, third over from the left. She was seventeen at the time, like most of her classmates. She's still smiling, as are her cohort.

These would have been shot in the autumn of 1942. Now the country was at war. Many of her classmates had been shipped to Manzanar six months earlier. Her smile, and the smiles of her senior classmates, betrays none of this. Life goes on. But those kids from the class of 1943 knew things the seniors from the previous year, smiling in the face of a merciless calendar, did not.

Remembrance: Manzanar

The young girl who rode her bike on December 7 was to find privacy banished, too. She remembered rows of toilets without partitions or doors, an area for the showers without curtains. At least men and women had separate shower facilities. As for the dining hall: cafeteria style, of course. Much of the younger set ate with friends, not with their families. A small detail, perhaps, given the big story of high desert exile more than a thousand miles from their green island. Not even a minor footnote in the books — that, for some, the tight family circle was weakened.

Resistance

The "fortunes of war," when they pivoted,
brought talk of the Nikkei's return.
Most letter writers to the *Review* wanted them back.
Not all. A man with a crackpot economics book to his name:
"We knew them as neighbors," wrote the No Return leader,
"as the smiling and inscrutable operators
of truck farms and grocery stores."
Then came his raw racism, those excremental words
ready and waiting in unlit cellars.

Then came the public meetings,
the first attended by two hundred. Applause
erupted when one claimed Indian reservations
a fit precedent for sending their neighbors off.
But the economics author cautioned his allies
against boycotting advertisers in the *Review*.
The *Review* must be kept in business, he said —
otherwise who will print our letters to the editor?
The gods of free speech could only blink.

Return, No Return

Release came. Fewer Japanese Americans
returned to their Northwest and California homes
than those from Bainbridge.

Mob violence broke out in Hood River, Oregon.
Seattle Teamsters prevented Japanese American produce
from reaching public markets.

Assorted West Coast newspapers whipped up
No Return froth. Houses left vacant
stood vandalized, their fields overgrown.

Far fewer No Return voices were raised on Bainbridge.
On Bainbridge there were those who had cared
for abandoned houses, possessions and fields.

The *Review* had done its job: The *Review*
had kept neighbors in touch through the long, dark night.
The No Returners, fists shoved in pockets, got on with life.

The watched-over fields fruited again.

In memory of Everett Thompson

I Knew

A child gazing up at adults knows things
beyond the words a child can make. I knew which
grown-ups wished them gone or raised their voices
against their return. I overheard my parents
say their names. My grandmother, who didn't
mince words, simply pointed. So I watched those lunar
faces in town, at the store, on the ferry,
their children my schoolmates. They who had been
demigods stood naked, their nimbus
no longer pure as my first communion host.
And I remembered the old priest who proffered
the wafer between tobacco-stained fingers
as he reached down through a world of shadow
and light where I too must walk.

A Music

William Faulkner: "The past is not dead. It's not even past."

The music of what happens
seeps into our buried lives.
For those who hear it
the world shines through the motes
in their own eyes.

They are the receivers of wisdom's wine,
say the old books, which fills
drop by difficult drop
the cup that accompanies those
who walk the humble road

of what must be done
to assume the invisible garments
of their better angels
until their body's slow seasons
burn bright against oblivion.

To Walt and Milly Woodward and to Bainbridge Island's unsung heroes who
looked after farms and fields and business affairs, and welcomed their neighbors
home.

Unmapped

Newspaper headlines, cafe colloquies,
telegrams, radio reports and movie-house newsreels —

the graffiti History's boarding-house-reach
forever leaves behind after the ransack of silence

deeper-down than ourselves. Maps, troop movements,
beribboned generals, strategies, victory and defeat —

Sunday histories recorded ten thousand feet above Monday.
It's all in the books. Except Monday's wound.

Remembrance: Future Tense

Many years later she looked back and wondered what kind of lessons had been taught to younger generations. She was a young woman, beyond high school, when she stepped on board the ferry Kehloken.

She looked back and saw respect for people as the most important thing, no matter their politics or skin color. At the time she remembered, the Exclusion Memorial lay in the planning stages. She hoped visitors to the site would undergo an emotional experience potent enough to provoke the same reaction far into the future as it would on the day of their visit. Based on respect.

Respect: from the Middle French, "respecter," used in English from the middle 1500s on as meaning "treating with regard or esteem."

"In Twelfth Night" Shakespeare went straight to the point with a question that might haunt the air at the Memorial today: "Is there no respect of place, persons, nor time with you?"

A life question.

In old age, the woman who looked back urged the answer must be yes, and that it be found in a quiet place on Bainbridge Island where a dock once stood.

In 2002

Today, on the Eagledale side of Eagle Harbor, a memorial wall commemorates the forced removal of 227 Japanese American men, women and children in the place where they boarded the ferry Kehloken for Seattle. The dock is gone.

On the sixtieth anniversary of that day, March 30, 2002, a cloudy Saturday morning, some 500 people gathered on the site of the future wall, then in the planning stages, to remember. The touchstone for the proceedings: *Nidoto Nai Yoni.* "Let It Not Happen Again."

The crowd stood while two-dozen or so Nikkei camp veterans, mostly gray-haired, shoulders bent by the years, sat on folding chairs down front and listened with the patience associated with Japanese culture. A few got up to speak, softly, with restraint.

One man, a dentist and a young child then, was a little more demonstrative: "Down this road we walked in shock. We didn't know where we were going."

A visiting pastor spoke of the soul's brokenness, as if the soul were a limb. "We are here to re-member," he said. Politicians had their say. One recalled Lincoln eyeballing the Other: "I don't like that man. I'll have to get to know him better." Washington's governor, of Chinese ancestry, said: "I don't like the word internment. It was imprisonment."

Heartfelt words were day-lighted that morning, and yet they couldn't quite touch the unsunned wells of our lives. Official proceedings have their limits. So does language.

Near the end, though, something changed.

A tall, dignified man in his mid-70's spoke — an Island old-timer of Scandinavian descent who served in the Pacific during the war. He started off telling funny stories about his Japanese American high school pals. That got the crowd laughing. Then he shifted to March 30, 1942, and started to

37

remember how it was in the place where we now stood. His voice started to flutter like a wounded dove, then shut down, and he wept.

In the crowd, heads lowered, as did the heads of the Japanese Americans sitting down front. As he struggled to regain himself, heads stayed down. The small waves behind him broke quietly on the mudflats. A robin caroled high in a fir. The choked silence lasted longer than was comfortable. This was sufficient.

At the end, a dignitary pulled the covering off a large rock where the head of the old dock stood. Its plaque tells the story of March 30, 1942.

As the sun broke through, the crowd sang "America the Beautiful."

Mary, at 88

Her living room fills with December dusk
where we drink the chewy Merlot I brought
to mark the festal season.

Only the low table light is turned on,
letting the first stars come to the window.
We've already talked an hour,

shaken our sticks at the Island's newcomers
and laughed. Much laughter.
She will see this Christmas but not another.

Of her childhood friend, my mother:
"She was always the leader. And she swam
in that cold water longer than anybody."

I ask about the grandmother handing out oranges
on the eve of the departures.
Did I remember the story right? I did.

And her father who lit the dock lights?
"My grandfather. On Sundays he made spaghetti.
Your mother showed up often to avoid pot roast at home."

She takes the bottle, not quite empty.
"Let's not leave anything on the table."
And Mary measures out, slowly, what there is.

The Bainbridge Island Japanese American Exclusion Memorial

A green salient
where a carefully placed needle
plays the gramophone of silence.

The curved memorial wall of old growth, red cedar,
granite and basalt, its five terra cotta friezes,
tells the story of this place
and follows the route walked to the ferry Kehloken.

Enshrined: The names and ages
of those who took only what they could carry.
And the repeated words:
Nidoto Nai Yoni. Let it not happen again.

And this:
"May the spirit of this memorial
inspire each of us to safeguard
constitutional rights for all."

The Memorial: December

The stars come into their own
over Eagledale with the silent
integrity of the dead

who wait deep in the dark
for the old stories to be told
so they might walk again with the living.

Stories we carry together like lanterns
as far as we can go
into the starlit night.

the Memorial —
a starlit tide breaks against
this shore of silence

About the Author

Mike Dillon's Bainbridge Island roots reach back four generations. He lives in Indianola, Washington, a small town on Puget Sound a few miles north of Bainbridge and twelve miles northwest of Seattle.

Four previous books of his poetry have been published by Bellowing Ark Press, including "That Which We Have Named," (2008). Red Moon Press has published three books of his haiku. Several of his haiku were included in "Haiku in English: The First Hundred Years," W.W. Norton (2013).

He is a retired publisher of community newspapers, a field he entered inspired by the example of Walt and Milly Woodward.

Acknowledgements

Eight of these poems, since revised, were published in "Current."

The prose passage, "In 2002," revised for this volume, was originally published in my book, "That Which We Have Named," (Bellowing Ark Press - 2008), where it appeared under the title "Where Words End."

The best-known book based on what happened on Bainbridge Island after Pearl Harbor is David Guterson's "Snow Falling on Cedars." The novel's central character is modeled on *Bainbridge Review* publisher and editor Walt Woodward, who died in 2001.

Woodward's daughter, Mary, has written the indispensible history of what happened on Bainbridge Island after Pearl Harbor. "In Defense of Our Neighbors," (2008) also makes clear the strong role her mother, Milly, played as events unfolded—Walt and Milly Woodward formed a close, working partnership. "In Defense" is a moving fusion of immaculate research, honest reporting and striking photographs. It is also the springboard for a number of the poems and passages in "Departures."

The Bainbridge Island Historical Museum provides an invaluable resource for learning more about the imprisonment of the Island's Nikkei population (those of Japanese ancestry), an event which serves as the quiet hinge of the Island's history.

The oral histories found on the Bainbridge Island Japanese American Community (BIJAC) website inspired the italicized "Remembrance" sections. The groundbreaking (1985) PBS documentary, "Visible Target," which, after long silence, got the public conversation about the "evacuations" moving, is also available on the BIJAC website.

Another BIJAC link leads to the Bainbridge Island Japanese American Exclusion Memorial pages. There is no substitute, however, for standing where the events of March 30, 1942 unfolded.

About the Press

Unsolicited Press was founded in 2012. The team strive to publish outstanding fiction, poetry, and creative nonfiction. Learn more at unsolicitedpress.com.

CPSIA information can be obtained
at www.ICGtesting.com
Printed in the USA
FSHW011122040919
61608FS

9 781947 021778